PILLARS OF THE REPUBLIC

FIVE ESSAYS ON THE FOUNDATIONAL PRINCIPLES OF OUR REPUBLIC AND ITS PRESERVATION

CHRISTOPHER HOLLRAH

authorHOUSE

AuthorHouse™
1663 Liberty Drive
Bloomington, IN 47403
www.authorhouse.com
Phone: 833-262-8899

Published by AuthorHouse 07/16/2024

ISBN: 979-8-8230-1039-9 (sc)
ISBN: 979-8-8230-1047-4 (e)

Library of Congress Control Number: 2023911297

Print information available on the last page.

Any people depicted in stock imagery provided by Getty Images are models, and such images are being used for illustrative purposes only. Certain stock imagery © Getty Images.

This book is printed on acid-free paper.

CONTENTS

DEDICATION

This book has several dedications

First, it is dedicated to my daughter. Please never lose the spark of the love of life in your eyes. This world is full of wonder, and you are the source of all of my joy.

Second, it is dedicated to every person, anywhere, in the past, present, or future who has, is, or will struggle and fight to defend the system of open and democratic republics everywhere. Millions of people have laid down their lives to help preserve and propel this form of government that functions on the democratic process, and to all of you, we owe a debt of gratitude that we can never repay. At this writing, the courageous people of Ukraine deserve our support in any manner possible. They, more than almost any other nation on this planet, are on the front lines of humanity's fight against dictatorship.

Third, it is dedicated to my father, who lived a life of intellectual vibrance, but who, in his later years, drifted into conservative extremism, which was warped and fed by his addiction to fox news (lower case intentional), which then took him, so easily it seemed, into the clutches of trumpism and acceptance of conspiracy theories. This tragedy helped created the need for this book.

Oh, yeah, and Jeff, whose assistance has been invaluable.

INTRODUCTION

This book contains five essays on what I feel are some of the most important philosophical principles which serve as foundations of the form of government that we, as Americans, along with billions of other people on this planet are privileged to enjoy; republicanism. It is important to specify that I am not just speaking about any nation-state that has the word 'republic' in its official title. This is not a delineator of republicanism.

Examples such as the People's Republic of China, the Democratic People's Republic of Korea, or the Islamic Republic of Iran will alert any reader to the fact that incorporating the word 'republic' into the name of your state means nothing. In fact, if you look around the world, I think you will find that it is a common practice for dictatorships of all kinds, religious, civil, or military, to use the word 'republic' in their official state name.

When I use the terms 'republic,' or 'republicanism,' I am speaking of a republic that functions on the democratic process in which elections are open and transparent, participation, either as a candidate for office or merely a voter is free to all citizens, and in which the process and results are fairly contested. This is where the difference lies between a dictatorship that abuses the term 'republic,' and a true republic that honors it.

The essays that appear in this manuscript are, in order of appearance: The Marketplace of Ideas, Freedom of Conscience, Secularism, Presumption of Innocence Before the Law, and The

Rule of Law. This is, by no means, an exhaustive list of those principles, developed and refined during the Age of Enlightenment and Reason which served as the building blocks that gave rise to the modern liberal republic, but they are, in my opinion, five of the most important principles that enabled the republican form of government to make the all important transition from a theoretical proposition, to a practical application when it was adopted at the birth of the United States in its Constitution.

In brief, each of the essays explores the following topics: The Marketplace of Ideas reviews the all-important place that this very concept plays in the maintenance of a free society, and how we have moved over farther from a society that cherishes it. Freedom of Conscience looks at how the individual must always be free to think and believe whatever they want, but this freedom of thought and belief does not and cannot translate to freedom of action. Secularism explores the essential need for a complete and total separation of the church and the state. Presumption of Innocence Before the Law discusses how this principle relates to contemporary American society, and how our accepted social practices, especially in policing, completely violate this foundational principle. Lastly, The Rule of Law, delves into this all important principle, both as a broad principle as it relates to how a society evolves and functions, as well as its timely application as we see the mounting evidence of a former president convicted of numerous felonies, and who is still under investigations for multiple felonious breaches of law elsewhere.

Over time, the concept of republicanism has evolved and spread throughout the world, and in this process, it has taken on differing forms adapted to the history and cultural landscape of the nations which have adopted it. However, republicanism has found its deepest roots and greatest expression in what is known as the European West and the United States, a political and cultural area commonly referred to as The West. It was the political philosophers of this massive geographical region that laid the foundations of what we now know as "modern liberal republicanism."

We must remember, though, that for all of its benefits regarding the liberation of the rights and responsibilities of the individual, the modern liberal republic is not without a dark side, and it is in no way immune to the drives of imperialism and colonialism, and it has, in no manner, served to mitigate the greed of both individuals and organizations. One of the worst expressions of the dark side of modern liberal republicanism, especially in United States foreign policy, is the absolutely epitomized expression of cultural arrogance: Nation Building.

This belief in the political and cultural superiority of the West has produced nothing but horrific results, both for the United States, the major global power that incorporated it into both its military and diplomatic foreign policy, and even more so for the nations of those countries what were subjected to this arrogance. How many dead Afghans and Iraqis are there in the world today because this republic, like some god, thought it could create subservient client states in its own image?

I do not intend to offer any sort of exposé on policies such as nation building in this book, as this is not the proper venue for such a discussion. I mention it solely to illustrate that republicanism as a form of government that functions on the democratic process, does not exist within a fantasy-laden vacuum of delightful benefits for those who live under its umbrella. Republics, just like monarchies and dictatorships, exist within the universe of power politics, and like monarchies and dictatorships, they are susceptible to the excesses born of human greed.

In the end, however, I hold the truth to be self-evident that republicanism and the democratic processes which mark its true expression possess within it the potential to release the energies of human goodness that are of such great value to humanity as a whole, that the sooner it spreads to all nations of this world, not through nation building imposed by an external power, but through natural cultural evolution, the safer, more secure, and more equitable will be the world in which we all live.

THE MARKETPLACE OF IDEAS

The market place of ideas, as a foundational principle of the "Modern Liberal Republic," may very well be the original founding principle envisioned during the Age of Enlightenment. The intellectual search was for a practical means by which to insure that the laws that govern any society were developed and informed through healthy, open and unrestricted debate, shifting coalitions, and compromise. More specifically, other foundational principles, both those discussed in this book and others not incorporated herein, evolved in order to support the search for a means by which to incorporate the marketplace of ideas into the foundation of any society existing under a single government.

By its very nature, any real marketplace of ideas must originate from the nation as a whole, and not from the elites that form the inner circle of government. As such, the concept of the marketplace of ideas did not fit well into the monarchical system of government known first-hand to the philosophers and political activists of the Age of Enlightenment and Reason. This marketplace and influence was restricted to the monarchs and their ministers who were bound by oath to serve the monarch, not the people over whom the monarch ruled.

Because this important relationship existed in this form, the market place of ideas consisted almost exclusively of the monarch's ideas, and the monarch's ideas were generally centered upon preservation of the rule of the monarch and the perpetuation of the monarchy as a whole. Also, because this relationship of ministers bound to the monarch does not exist in the modern liberal republic, Donald Trump's series of efforts to illegally remain in office after losing the 2020 presidential election failed. They failed because the people who worked either within the executive branch of government, or actually in the White House itself, took very seriously the oath they swore to defend our Constitution against all enemies, both foreign and domestic. Donald Trump and his MAGA sycophants in congress are domestic enemies of this republic and our Constitution.

The political philosophers who applied their intellectual abilities to the very development of the modern liberal republic somehow foresaw many of the dangers we now face. They foresaw not only the attempts to combine the powers of the church and the state, but also to brand a free press as the enemy of the people. Needless to say, the marketplace of ideas needs to be resurrected on a global scale and on a national scale here in the United States in particular. As I shall say in the concluding remarks, education will be the key.

For the record, we should review exactly what Donald Trump's illegal series of efforts entailed. There were eight separate efforts by Trump and his allies to overturn the will of the American electorate and Joe Biden's victory in the 2020 presidential election. Though most of these efforts overlap to some extent, the following list is in chronological order:

- The Trump campaign filed numerous lawsuits to try to overturn the election results. All failed, and most were thrown out due the lack of any substantive evidence.

- Trump and his allies empaneled false sets of electors to try to disrupt and obstruct the work of Congress.
- Trump tried to pressure state-level officials and legislatures to not certify the valid results of the voting in their states.
- Trump tried to pressure republicans in both houses of the United States Congress to refuse to certify the results of the voting of the electoral college.
- Trump tried to pressure Vice President Mike Pence to refuse to certify the votes of the electoral college.
- Trump tried to weaponize the Department of Justice to claim that massive voter fraud had taken place in the 2020 presidential election.
- Trump tried engage to United States military to forcibly seize voting machines throughout the country and claim that they were rigged to switch votes from Trump to Biden.
- Trump planned and incited the insurrection and attempted coup d'état to try to forcefully prevent Congress from certifying the votes of the electoral college.

I will return to the central focus of this portion of this essay now, but I thought that it was important that the reader have a catalog of the actual plots employed by Trump to overthrow the American government and retain power illegally.

In the twenty-first century, it is primarily the civil and religious dictatorships populating our globe that exclude the marketplace of ideas from their systems of government, and there are still a handful of monarchies that deny their 'subjects' the right to this basic principle of fair and equitable governance. These dictatorships and hold-over monarchies exist in an environment of constant and pervasive fear of all of the foundational principles of republicanism, and of the marketplace of ideas in particular.

Knowing this, it is easy to understand why suppressing the marketplace of ideas by dictatorial governments is essential to their survival. These governments understand that if they were to allow the marketplace of ideas to flourish among the people over whom they rule, the first idea expressed would be the elimination of the dictatorial government in favor of some form of a modern liberal republic.

In this regard, I am reminded of the serious, yet somewhat humorous remarks of Thomas Paine from his tract *"The Rights Of Man:"*

> *"If there existed a man so transcendently wise above all others that his wisdom was necessary to instruct a nation, some reason might be offered for monarchy; but when we cast our eyes about a country, and observe how every part understands its own affairs; and when we look about the world, and see that of all men in it, the race of kings are the most insignificant in capacity, our reason cannot fail to ask us— what are those men kept for?"*

That statement expresses very succinctly the danger to monarchy and dictatorship which the marketplace of ideas poses.

Like most people who live lives in the world of unashamed adulthood, I have done my best to continually move toward some semblance of that which is 'truth.' I wish I could have stated "Like everyone who lives a life…," but I cannot, for this does not seem to be the truth. Many people, and I have evidence to support my claim, find the search for ever greater and deeper truths in their life to be more trouble than it is worth. They have half inherited half constructed for themselves a universe that works — well enough.

We must also remember that a statement can only become what we know as a cliché if it bears an essential truth within it, and the ancient cliché that "ignorance is bliss" is true at its core. In this cliché lies the reason many people give up the search for truth; "Why be troubled and thoughtful, when you can be happy? Leave that search to young people. I've had all the truth I can stand for one life." Unfortunately, this strange don't-worry-be-happy-as-self-preservation approach to adulthood creates a problem, not only for the individual who adopts it as their modus vivendi, but for humanity as a whole.

It also poses a threat to the republics of which these people are citizens. It poses this threat because the modern liberal republic requires its citizens to be engaged with the world around them. In order for this form of government to thrive, the citizens must understand that it is their dedication to the principles that are the foundation of the modern liberal republic, and their participation in the democratic process, which will propel the republic into the future. Disengagement, on the other hand, carries within it the seeds of both the republic's demise and the dictatorship that will replace it. The only effective defense any republic has is the dedication of each individual citizen and resident to the foundational principles that gave it life in the first place.

In this personal search for what is true, I have developed the following means of proceeding on my journey. I take a critical look at what I believe, that which I have held to be true, and assume that I am wrong. From this point I can then look at opposing positions from the fresh perspective that perhaps they represent truth. This intellectual and spiritual exercise, though focused at times on a single issue, is really a continuous affair in the lives of those who commit themselves to never stopping the search for truth. It is generally characterized by a simultaneous constant search, on a subconscious level, for new truths that will both form and inform our personal universe.

This entire lifestyle of seeking truth, even in the most uncommon and uncomfortable places and circumstances, is not the shallow bliss that purposeful ignorance will bring. Rather, it is a deeper and more satisfying happiness that resides in the core of one's being. I am also convinced that this search for truth is one of the subconscious drives of life, whereas living in willful ignorance is to live in a constant state of destructive inner conflict in which the soul seeks truth and knowledge, but the consciousness constantly denies it satisfaction.

⚬⟨❦⟩⚬

In my never-ending search for what is true, I have long maintained that the greatest enemy of the political right in this country is the marketplace of ideas, and the evidence to support this view is very strong. I have held this view while also believing that the marketplace of ideas is not the enemy of the political left, and once again the evidence in support of this is just as strong. You don't have to spend much time in the United States of America to realize the truth of this — at least that it is partially true.

Since I have believed (and still do) that the marketplace is the sworn enemy of the political right wing in this country, I will offer my evidence in support of this belief. It is in those states controlled by the modern neo-republican party, that several policy stances which offer supportive evidence of my contention have become law. These include, but are in no way limited to, the following:

- Restrictions on women's access to critical health care
- Banning of books
- Refusal to increase the scope of state assisted health care
- Opposition to initiatives to protect the planet and combat climate change
- Opposition to regulations setting a minimum standard of conduct for corporations
- Defunding public education
- Overfunding police forces
- Racist and white ethnocentric immigration policies
- Laws restricting personal expression by members of the LGBTQ+ community

As I stated, this is not an exhaustive list of the legal structures created in various states controlled by the neo-republican party. Not only have they enacted laws in support of the agenda above, but they have also changed the rules the citizens of that state must follow in order to create ballot initiatives that would allow the people of that state to make their actual voices heard on these issues. In each case, they have made it more difficult for the residents of those states to affect the political system through their own voices. This is an undeniable indicator of a fear of the marketplace of ideas.

I have also believed (and still do) that the marketplace of ideas is not the enemy of the political left. In each case, the left opposes the restrictive and backward-looking policies above, and I think it is self-evident that support for women's rights, policies combating climate change, a more egalitarian view of the world and its peoples, and a host of other initiatives opposed by the right wing is where the marketplace of ideas resides. However, I think that there is a problem with this analysis, and the problem lies with the concept that the marketplace of ideas is not the enemy of the left; specifically, the institutional left.

On April 20th and 21st, 2024, I was on the campus of the University of Southern California attending the Los Angeles Times Festival of Books. If you are a sentient being at all, then you know that it was impossible to be in that environment, at that time, and not find yourself in the middle of the controversy that was, in large measure, the genesis of the nationwide campus protests of the spring of 2024.

The Valedictorian for the graduating class of 2024 is a young woman named Asna Tabassum. She is Muslim and has a definitive pro-Palestinian political stance. Once it was determined that she would deliver a commencement address, several pro-Israeli groups objected to her being able to deliver her remarks and threatened violence if she was allowed to speak at commencement. The university administration bowed to pressure from these groups and their threats, and announced that they were forbidding Ms. Tabassum the privilege she had earned through her academic achievements to address her graduating class and the assembled faculty, administrators, and guests at commencement.

The groups that threatened violence if Ms. Tabassum was allowed to speak — to immerse herself and all people present in the marketplace of ideas — did not know what her remarks would contain; all they knew was that there was a very good chance that she would remind her classmates that it is their right, no, their duty to fight for liberty and justice for all in this world, regardless of who those people might be.

The pro-Israeli groups that threatened to bring violence into the sacred ceremony of commencement understood only that there was a chance that she would remind the students and guests present that the Palestinian people have been living under more than seventy years of harsh military occupation by the state of Israel, and that as she spoke, the people of Gaza were being subjected to a systematic genocide inflicted upon them with a malice of intent not yet seen in the twenty-first century.

What this incident awakened in me was the realization of the disconnect that resides within the political left in this country, and yet does not present itself as a problem for the political right. Both the institutional interests and the rank and file members of the political right do not experience a disconnect in the message they have for America. The MAGA movement, under the banner of support for the political aspirations of donald trump is unified in its message. Their actual interests differ, but both groups are unified on almost every important point of policy and law in this country. This is because all other interests and voices of dissent against the MAGA neo-republican party hierarchy have either been effectively silenced, or actually removed from their offices within the party .

This lack of visible and functional disagreement in the political right may seem like a beneficial aspect to its adherents, but it is not. It is actually detrimental to the political aspirations of its members since debate, coalition building, compromise, and the marketplace of ideas have all been eliminated from its internal processes. This has caused a hardening of the party's positions on important issues, as well as a drift further and further to the right. Eventually, the republican party, the primary institution of conservative positions in American politics, will publicly embrace the white supremacy, neo-nazi, and white christian nationalist agendas; something it has done on a tacit level already, and all of which seek the destruction of this republic.

This does not bode well for many of its candidates for political office, because no matter how hardened and extreme a person's views my seem in a verbal exchange with others, when it comes to voting behavior, people tend to choose candidates closer to the center. It will not negatively affect candidates in backwater right wing christian grottos like Oklahoma, but candidates who must compete for offices in parts of this country in which civilization still has a place in civic life will find it difficult to win their contests.

That is the problem that the right wing in this country has; a lack of disagreement on the direction in which the movement should proceed. Perhaps it is not that there is absolutely no dissent within the republican party, the problem, as I stated above, is that all dissent from the trumpist, MAGA wing has been effectively silenced. The result has been that for all dominating groups within the republican party, the marketplace of ideas is their enemy.

The problem the left has is both different and, to be honest, more healthy. The left in this country has a definitive disagreement and disconnect within its ranks on the direction in which the movement and the democratic party should proceed. The democratic party and the leftist movement in general is divided into what have become known as the progressive wing and the Wall Street wing. The Wall Street wing of the democratic party is, in many ways, the centrist wing of the party, but more so in their approach to corporate involvement in politics than their definitive policy preferences. As such, the Wall Street wing of the democratic party represents the status quo institutional left.

However, the elected and appointed officials, and other operatives within this group understand that a vast majority of rank and file members of the democratic party have much more progressive views than they do on almost every issue confronting our nation, and so they espouse support for initiatives like the Green New Deal. Herein lies the healthy disconnect within the political left; the progressive wing and the Wall Street wing of the democratic party continually compete for advantage in an environment of mutual respect, and an internal knowledge that they both seek a better America.

The Wall Street wing's status as representatives of the age old status quo in American politics keeps them bound to the dark money flowing through the veins of our body politic. As such, the marketplace of ideas is their enemy.

❧

We are now at the point in this essay in which I tell you that much of what I have written prior to this point is false. I'm sorry, but that is part and parcel of a life lived in the constant search for truth. Throughout my considerations for the content of this essay, I have come to realize that the marketplace of ideas, in and of itself, is not the enemy of the rank and file right or left.

Personally, I find the marketplace from which the rank and file right draws its ideas for what they consider appropriate to guide the social norms and the laws of this country to be absolutely repulsive. They are fascistic and support the imposition of a white christian evangelical theocratic dictatorship, with the executive authority placed in the hands of donald trump. The intended affect of this is the destruction of this republic and the liberal and egalitarian principles upon which it was founded, and that have propelled it from its inception to the present day.

As horrendous as this sounds (and is), it is still an exploration of the marketplace of ideas, and those of us who truly value the principles upon which this republic was founded, must grant all persons the freedom of conscience to which all people have a right. We cannot allow these dreams of white dictatorship to come to fruition, but we must allow those that think and believe such things the freedom to do so, while vehemently decrying these ideas as what they are: counter to everything American.

The left, of course, explores its own version of this marketplace, and some of their ideas are just as repulsive to the essence of a republic that functions on the democratic process as those described above. The extreme left, in the United States, represented by the CPUSA, Communist Party in the USA, holds some rather extreme views on the direction of this country, but the CPUSA is still a very small portion of the political left in this country, and their calls for a dictatorship of the proletariat go largely unnoticed in large sections of our country, as well as among their colleagues on the political left within both wings of the democratic party. Please remember also, that the CPUSA and any splinter groups that come from it, are separate political parties, and are not part of the democratic party.

The difference, here, lies in the fact that the ideas of the extreme left remain on the fringe of left-wing consciousness and play no part in the development of the national platform of the Democratic Party, whereas the ideas of the extreme right now form the basis of mainstream right-wing thought in America, and control the development of the national platform of the Republican Party. So, both the rank and file adherents to the political philosophies of the left and the right appreciate access to the marketplace of ideas. How, then, have we arrived at a point in the history of this republic in which the marketplace of ideas has been replaced by the marketplaces of celebrity gossip, and purposeful disinformation?

Money and its entrenched interests.

The marketplace of ideas is the enemy of the wealthy and the powerful on this planet. Any seemingly novel idea that arises out of the nation to move society forward toward greater equality, a more fair and equitable distribution of wealth, and greater inclusion in the economic and political life of this world will be immediately assessed by these forces to determine whether or not it can be played to their monetary advantage. If it cannot be manipulated in such a manner, then it will be squashed. This was the essential discovery I made while considering this foundational principle of republicanism after my trip to Los Angeles, and my experiences on the USC campus in particular.

This is why we have left any semblance of anything even remotely close to a society interested in the marketplace of ideas, and have entered the age of the marketplace of celebrity gossip, and the marketplace of disinformation. The forces of wealth want each and every one of us to be unconcerned with the political health of our republic and more concerned with the internal squabbles of the royal family in England.

Just as the marketplace of ideas was the enemy of monarchs prior to the rise of republicanism in the West, so it is the enemy of dictatorships in the world today. A prime example of this is how the Chinese Communist Party has strangled the infusion of the ideas of liberty and freedom in the People's Republic through its nearly absolute control of people's access to information through the internet.

However, make no mistake, the marketplace of ideas is also the sworn enemy of the institutional and wealthy interests in free societies, and as we move toward ever greater normalization of the mechanisms of social control, we run the risk of mirroring dictators like Xi in China, and Putin in Russia.

The answer to how we move back into the age of the marketplace of ideas is not an easy question to answer, and I do not currently have one that does not involve extreme social upheaval. The core of our problem stems from the fact that the interests of the wealthy and powerful control the vast majority of media in the world today, and media of all sorts is now so tightly woven into the fabric of our daily lives, that each individual would have to accept major changes in the nature and amount of its presence.

Can anyone actually accept completely shutting down Fox News, Newsmax, Info Wars, and the Trinity Broadcasting Network, to name just four of the most poisonous media outlets in the United States today? From a certain, Machiavellian perspective, yes, but from a perspective that honors the foundational principles of our republic, no.

Once again, as I say so many times, the major part of our recovery for a republic on the brink of life support, and that is in danger of going 'flatline,' is education. We must educate our children, from the earliest years, in the principles of liberty and equality and continue this education through their adolescence. This is not done through immersing them in "patriotic" activities, but through educating them in principles, and developing within each and every one of them the sharpest critical thinking skills of any population on our planet.

Automaton-like activities like flag worship, designed solely to create little patriots, eventually leads to acceptance of phrases like "my country, right or wrong." Statements like that build dictatorships, not healthy republics. Our children must be raised with the attitude of "my country when it's right, but I stand against it when it's wrong." Statements like that build healthy republics, and forge an impenetrable bulwark against the infectious disease of dictatorship.

If we do not begin, now, to educate our children in the principles outlined in this book; a respect for the marketplace of ideas, the value of freedom of conscience, the essential requirement of secularism, that all people are presumed innocent before the law, and that the rule of law must be supreme in this country, then the lamp for the world that this imperfect republic has been will soon be extinguished.

FREEDOM OF CONSCIENCE

This piece is dedicated to what I believe is one of the most important foundational principles of the modern liberal republic, Freedom of Conscience, and I find it worth noting that the principles which form the basis of modern liberal republicanism, five of which I discuss in this book, were developed during the Age of Enlightenment in the 17th and 18th centuries in both Europe and America.

Also, some of the most important things I try to illuminate for the people who are reading this book, read my essays on my blog site, overwhelmingweirdness.com, and perhaps also watch the related humorous videos on my YouTube channel, Artlife Enterprises, are the whole set of concepts that are essential to the republican form of government. To be clear, I am not talking about government by the republican party, but modern liberal republicanism as a form of government; what I often refer to as "a republic that functions on the democratic process." I also know that many conservatives who are reading this essay just cringed at the mention of the word "liberal," but just as "republican form of government" has nothing to do with the republican party, so use of the term "liberal" here has nothing to do with the contemporary democratic party in the United States.

Simply stated, my definition of Freedom of Conscience is the following:

The individual must always, at all times, and under all circumstances be free, without legal consequence to think whatever they want. Likewise, the individual must also always, at all times, and under all circumstances, be free, without legal consequence, to believe whatever they want.

This is freedom of conscience, and it lies at the very center of what is known as liberal republicanism as a form of government. It shares this central place with the marketplace of ideas, secularism, presumption of innocence before the law, and the rule of law, which I discuss in the other essays in this book.

In my view, it is essential to the survival of any republic that freedom of conscience, these freedoms of thought and belief, no matter how righteous or perverse they may seem to any individual or group, are never regulated or limited in any manner, at any time. A person's freedom of conscience must be completely unregulated, for as soon as the state, or any other actors, such as religious institutions, assume the right to regulate what a person thinks or believes, the republic is no more, and the individual and the nation as a whole will have been rendered powerless.

However, freedom of conscience must be strictly limited to thought and belief. Freedom of conscience can never translate directly to freedom of action. The actions of the individual must always be regulated to some extent, for thought and belief exist solely within the vacuum of the individual, but action always exists within the world outside the individual. Actions always have the potential to affect others in both a positive or negative manner, and because of this, they must always be subject to some form of regulation.

Most of our actions seem as if they are unregulated, and this is because our actions generally exist within the accepted parameters of social norms, and legal restraints, but the necessary regulation is there. Whether the regulation is transparent or opaque, all actions of the individual, whether alone, or in concert with others are rightfully regulated within society. Even those actions to which we are guaranteed the right by our Constitution are regulated in some manner.

⋅⋅⋅∞⋅⋅⋅

One of the most important practical manifestations of the concept of freedom of conscience is that the state does not have the right to tell any individual who that individual's enemies are, whether they be foreign or domestic. This is something that the individual must always have the right to decide within the confines of their own conscience. All of us must have the right to make the decision as to who is and is not our enemy or our friend.

The state has the right inform the individual of those groups, both foreign and domestic, that it feels work either in agreement with, or counter to, the interests of the state or the nation, and hence the individual, but that is all it has the right to do. The state does not have the right to say to anyone; "These people are your enemies, or these people are your friends." Alas, regardless of the nature of any country's system of government, both the state and the church will, eventually, try to do just this. So rest assured, the basic human right of freedom of conscience will come under siege at some point in the life of this nation.

There is also a very practical manifestation to the point of this essay and the definition of freedom of conscience which I have just laid out, and it is a discussion of the application of freedom of conscience and regulation of action as it applies to the intertwined neo nazi, fascist, white supremacist, and white christian nationalist movements in America. These groups and their separate yet intertwined agendas, are often referred to as the "white power" movement, and I will refer to them as such from this point on in this book.

The very existence of the right of freedom of conscience means, by default, that the white power movement in America has every right to exist. Every single individual who thinks fascist and white supremacist thoughts, or seeks to impose a white evangelical christian theocratic dictatorship on this country while holding the core beliefs of the white power movement in their hearts and minds has the right to do so. They even have the right to freely and peaceably associate with each other. Furthermore, as part of the political process, the white power movement has the right to put up candidates for elected office.

I need to digress from my central focus for just a second, and tell you of what I have seen in American society. Like all children who experienced thirteen years in the American public school system, I was taught that America is a place where freedom of conscience exists. However, what I saw in the curriculum of my American history classes was that in Post-World War II America, people who held communist beliefs were being harassed in direct opposition to the principle of freedom of conscience. Also, if they were not actually being beaten, harassed, and arrested, they were denied, as much as possible, any opportunity to participate in the economy. Even as a child, I never understood this insanely blatant application of a double standard; that freedom of conscience exists in America for everyone, except...

Not only that, but America had just fought the most high-intensity conflict the world had ever seen, World War II, against fascism, and five years later we were arresting communists. Granted, the Soviet Union had risen as America's preeminent adversary in the quest for ideological domination on Earth, but to be honest, I don't ever remember a lesson plan in school, that included images or references to any fascists being subjected to violent treatment on a society-wide scale during the period from the late 1940's to the early 1960's. I don't think it happened. Perhaps this is because fascists, white supremacists, and the white power movement in general is, in the end, corporate friendly.

I apologize for that digression, but I thought it was relevant to any discussion of American socio-political philosophy and history as they relate to freedom of conscience. Let us return, then, to our focus, the current white power movement in America and how it relates to the freedom of conscience / regulation of action dichotomy. As I have stated, since we live in a secular republic in which each individual is believed to possess freedom of conscience, the white power movement has every right to exist, and all elements thereof; fascism, white supremacy, white christian nationalism, and others, as an allied, if not unified political belief, have the right to be part of our political system. This is a central element of the marketplace of ideas. That concept, the free and expanding marketplace of ideas, is essential if we are to succeed in our march toward a more perfect union.

Like republicans, democrats, libertarians, democratic socialists, the green party, whomever, fascists, neo-nazis, and white supremacists have the right to function peacefully within the democratic system. They have the right to put candidates forward for office, and they can advertise in those media outlets that will take their money and conduct business with them. These elements of the far right, like everyone else, have the right to think and believe whatever that want, but their actions to fulfill their designs to amass political power based upon those thoughts and beliefs are, and must be, regulated. As part of that, however, they should be regulated no more and no less than any other political viewpoint.

The white power movement has the right to function peacefully and respectfully within the democratic system.

Peacefully and respectfully.

Peacefully and respectfully.

What they do not have the right to do, is bring violence into our political system. Of course, neither does the left, but violence from the left is generally sporadic, impromptu, and narrowly targeted. As such, it is not well funded, or very well organized.

The argument put forward to me regarding the violence of the left during the summer of protest in 2020, has been, without fail: "Look at the violence in Portland, Oregon!" Allow me to respond to that diversionary tactic here. The violence of the left in Portland followed several days of peaceful protests in which the government, at the direction of Trump's weaponized justice department, began snatching protesters off of the streets, forcing them into unmarked vehicles, and taking them away, mysteriously, to unknown locations. They showed no identification, they did not indicate that the persons being kidnapped were guilty of any crime, other than exercising their First Amendment right to petition their government for redress of grievances. Federal law enforcement personnel simply grabbed them, stuffed them into black vans or SUVs, and sped off.

I don't care whether you are an American, or a citizen of any country in this world, and I don't care if you are on the political left, or the right, because when your government begins to do something like that, civil disobedience, in whatever measure, becomes the responsibility of every citizen, and I fail to see when and how that civil disobedience could become too extreme. So, yes, the people of Portland, Oregon began to physically attack the Federal Building in their city in response to the most illegal conduct by our government one can imagine. More power to them.

The violence from the right is not that. The violence of the right, emulating, in large measure from the ultra conservative, white power movement in America is constant, planned, broadly targeted, well funded, and well organized.

Violence, in varying degrees, has been a constant theme and a characteristic property of fascism and white supremacy throughout their histories. Today, in the United States of America, they are harassing school board members, threatening the lives of electoral system staff members and their families, threatening the lives of elected officials and their families, creating propaganda campaigns to raise doubts about the very validity of our electoral systems, and yes, staging a failed coup d'état. The white power movement, incorporating its elements of fascism, white supremacy, neo nazism, and white christian nationalism all routinely employ violence as part of their operational agenda.

To be sure, the actions cited in the last paragraph are an accurate description of what the far right is doing on a daily basis in America right now. This cannot be allowed. Their introduction of violence into the American political environment poses the greatest threat to our republic to date, and these groups have used the rise of the political career of Donald Trump as their spokesperson to announce their entrance into the body politic's visible spectrum.

Violence is one of the primary tools used by fascist movements in their effort to secure power, and it is used freely by white supremacist forces to retain what they see as having been their power in the past, expressed primarily as their station of white privilege. Adherents of the white power movement on a global scale routinely employ organized violence as a political tool, but what is even more dangerous for us as Americans is that they now also possess a political party; the republican party. Through this possession, and the well developed communication, fundraising, and political organization systems the republican party possesses, they are seeking to normalize violence as part of our political processes, making it so frequent that it becomes accepted political behavior in a republic that was born for the very purpose of operating on a democratic system of free and fair elections devoid of violence. To this end, the Republican National Committee, on February 4th, 2022, labeled the the deadly, attempted coup d'état at the United States Capitol on January 6th, 2021 "legitimate political discourse."

⁘

The question we must answer now, is how do we stand against the forces that are bringing violence into America's political culture? I suggest two means. First, of course, vote. Vote in every election. More importantly, vote for candidates who will stand beside the core principles of modern liberal republicanism, even if you disagree with them on policy. A politician can always be swayed somewhat on policy, for compromise by adults is how republicanism works and survives. Conversely, politicians can hopefully not be swayed to any degree on the sanctity of this republic and the liberal, foundational principles which gave it birth.

Second, engage in political discourse…like adults. I am convinced that one of the main reasons why we find ourselves in a situation in which we actually have an active and growing white power political movement in this country stems primarily from the right's forty-five year old war on education. If we are to keep this republic, we must find a way to transform ourselves into a nation that peacefully talks everyday civics, and the only way to do that is to fully fund our educational systems. We must also wrest our educational system from the forces that taken control of it, and have established a dislike and a distrust of the concept of knowledge without limits.

Our right to any meaningful degree of freedom of conscience

will pass away if we allow the forces of fascism and white supremacy to gain a foothold in our political system through their methods of violence. Not only can we not allow it, but we are the only people who can stop it. Let the white power movement exist; they have that right. Let them honestly place their beliefs and policy goals out in the marketplace of ideas; they have a right to that also. However, we cannot allow anyone, regardless of what they think or believe, to sweep aside the freedoms that make republicanism as a form of government what it is and can be, in exchange for their dreams of despotism.

A PILLAR OF REPUBLICANISM: SECULARISM

"The government of the United States is in no way founded on the Christian religion. The United States of America should have a foundation free from the influence of the clergy."

~ George Washington

In order to speak about secularism as a foundational principle of modern liberal republicanism, I need to talk about the historical relationship between the church and the state, and how that relationship both affects and relates to the nation and the individual. As a prelude to this, I will offer a few definitions:

The church: An institutional entity that seeks control over both the nation and the individual through manipulating people's visions of the nature and will of god, and seeks to exercise control of the individual's life through appeals to professed moral imperatives.

The state: An institutional entity that seeks control over the nation and the individual and exercises civil governance over both in a single society within a specific geographic area, and seeks control over the individual's life through appeals to patriotic duty.

The nation: That group of people who share a common historical experience, value structure, and basic set of moral parameters over which both the church and the state seek control within their prescribed spheres of influence.

The individual: A person who is a member of any nation and/or society within what is referred to as a 'nation state.' The individual need not me a member of the nation, per se, only a person who lives under the protection and jurisdiction of the state.

Under this set of definitions, we can understand that both the church and the state are, first, last, and always, institutions of control, and are the power structures that stand in opposition to the nation and the individual. For our purposes here in reference to contemporary American society, "the church" refers specifically to this society's politically dominant religious sect, and this encompasses the multiplicity of denominations which broadly comprise the fundamentalist evangelical protestant church.

The playing field of power between these two sets of actors has never been level, because it has always been two against one: the church and the state verses the nation, and within the nation, the individual. For centuries, the church and the state, in close collusion with one another, were able to completely subjugate the nation. The rise of modern, liberal republicanism changed that equation and may have actually leveled the playing field, because the nation and the individual, under the principles of modern liberal republicanism, are generally able to resist the ambitions of control of both the church and the state.

However, this loose alliance of convenience between the church and the state did not always exist. From the formation of the most primitive human governments, to the kingdoms of post-Medieval Europe, the church and the state made war against each other over absolute control of the population. The conflict was bitter and physical, with kings finding themselves condemned to hell by the church, and the lands and assets of the church being seized by the state. A number of high-ranking officials on both sides lost their lives in this centuries-long war, and all of it was for absolute control of the mass of peasants, artisans, and all others outside of the nobility and the priesthood.

Eventually, the church and the state in Europe, out of sheer necessity, came to terms, made peace, and split the spoils of social control. Instead of fighting one another for absolute, unlimited control, they joined forces and supported each other's control over a more limited segment of the individual's existence. This alliance has been demonstrated over the centuries through the practice of the head of nationally dominant churches placing the crown of authority on the heads of new monarchs.

The peace forged by the church and state, as durable as it has been, has always been marked by an intense distrust and dislike of one for the other. The church and the state both covet the power over the nation and individual which the other possesses. This, of course, begs the question "what, exactly, does each of them have?" The division was, and continues to be, marked out in the following manner: the state has control of the individual's life, and the church has control over the individual's view of death.

Unfortunately, for both the church and the state, the division of power over the separate spheres of the lives of both the nation and the individual in the peace they forged and have supported over the centuries, led to the birth of secularism as a sine qua non of modern liberal republicanism.

⸎

Amendment 1 to the Constitution of the United States

> *"Congress shall make no law respecting the establishment of religion, or prohibiting the free exercise thereof; or abridging the freedom of speech, or of the press, or of the right of the people to peaceably assemble, and to petition the government for a redress of grievances"*

The First Amendment to the Constitution begins with the prohibition of collaboration between the church and the state. It separates them, placing a wall between them. The church is not allowed to meddle in the affairs of the state, and the state is not allowed to meddle in the affairs of the church. In order to solidify this division, the state does not tax the church. The purpose of this practice is to remove the church from any interest in the the affairs of the state. Since the church pays no taxes to the state, it has no right to even attempt to influence the politics or policies of the state.

If you think for one second that the people who wrote our

Constitution did not see the immediate and severe threat that a politically active church would pose to the survival of any republic, then please answer one question: why did the first words of the First Amendment to our Constitution deal with the relationship between the church and the state? Why, also, did Article Six our Constitution, the last article that dealt with the structure of our government, end with the words; *"...no religious test shall ever be required as a Qualification to any Office or public trust under the United States?"* It is because they saw the danger in any sort of collusion between secular and religious institutions.

The political philosophers of the Enlightenment to which modern republicanism owes it origins had an awareness of history and events contemporary to them that seems to have been lost in the United States in the twenty-first century. Their awareness was based upon their own experience of the dangers posed by a politically active church. Because of this awareness on their part, secular republicanism is meant to limit the effect that both the church and the state have on each other, limit the effect and amount of control each has over the nation and the individual, and most importantly, eliminate to the greatest degree possible, the influence of the church on the political life of the nation and the individual. I understand that in the United States of America in the early twenty-first century, this separation is, at the very least, blurred, if not erased altogether, but that theory/practice dichotomy is not yet a subject of this essay.

Secular republicanism is, in some ways, the practical expression of the victory of the individual over the state and freedom of the individual from the church. What, then, are some of the practical applications of secularism as a pillar of republicanism? I have identified three very important aspects, or rules, regarding the relationship between the church and the state in a secular republic which I feel are critical to the proper and long-term functioning of a republic that operates on the democratic process.

Rule number one: The state cannot favor one religious sect over another.

> *"An alliance or coalition between government and religion cannot be too carefully guarded against."*
>
> -James Madison

The state cannot favor Islam over Judaism, just as it cannot favor any sort of polytheistic, or animistic religions over Christianity. The religions developed and chosen by human cultures to help people weave their way toward salvation and some form of personal unity with the universe and god are as numerous as the cultures themselves, and the state cannot discriminate between them.

This is not to say that the state cannot place limits on how religions practice their belief systems, but these limits must be very, circumspect. The state has the right and the responsibility to protect people from abuse by others, whether the abusers be secular in nature, religious leaders, or other devotees of the individual's faith, but it must always cast a wary eye on creating and enforcing limits on religious practice.

Consenting adults have the right to voluntarily subject themselves to all sorts of strange and bizarre acts in the pursuit of almost anything. It doesn't matter whether the goal is to bring them closer to god, or to orgasm, the state must stand afar and not intervene. However, when the circumstances move from consent to coercion, then the state may, and should, step in to protect the individual from abuse by anyone, especially the church. This is because, as an institution of social control, almost all religious sects can and will, if allowed, exercise incredibly intense forms of control over the individual, and they possess the tools to create a coercive environment from which the individual will find it extremely difficult, if not impossible to break free.

Further to this, the state must also seek to insure that a politically active church does not attempt to control the thoughts, beliefs and actions of any person who is not a voluntary member of that religious sect. This means that the state cannot allow religious sects to try to influence either constitutional or statutory law based upon their religious beliefs. Secularism means, above all, and in the briefest terms possible that "Your faith is your business. Keep it that way."

Rule number two: The state cannot use the nation's tax dollars to support the endeavors of any religious sect.

This act immediately violates rule number one, as the state cannot afford, unless it seeks to tax the nation into absolute poverty, to equally support the religious endeavors of every church or religious sect operating within the society over which it has governance. If the state uses the nation's tax revenue to support the endeavors of the church, it will inevitably favor one sect over all others, and this favoritism will then, inevitably, lead to collusion between that particular religious sect and the state, which will then, inevitably foster animosity between religious sects, which will then, inevitably lead to people hating one another.

Financial support of the church through use of the nation's tax revenue not only creates tacit, if not blatant support for that religious sect's belief system, but it alters that sect's dogma so that the church begins to support and validate the actions of the state as an extension of the will of god. Before too long, the nation will find itself saddled with a hybrid government that is no longer a secular republic free of religious interference, but one that is a partnership between the wealthiest secular interests in society, bolstered by a theocratic support system that subjugates the nation, and all individuals therein, into obedience under a non-democratic state.

Unless you are completely unaware of twenty-first century American history, you know that this rule has already been violated by the United States government. When President George W. Bush announced that the United States government would support the endeavors of various Christian denominations through what were called "faith-based initiatives" with the tax dollars of the American nation, I was appalled. This was a clear violation of one of the most important foundational principles of modern republicanism; the separation of the church and the state.

Likewise, if you think that there is not clear competition between religious sects in any society, then you have not eyes to see, nor ears to hear. Each new devotee represents an increase in the profitability of that sect. Any religious sect which has the financial backing of the state gains an immediate advantage in the acquisition of new devotees over other sects. This financial association gives them not only the freedom to spend their revenue on increasing the size of their congregations, but it also allows them to advertise their sect as preferred by the state, and tie their dogma to hollow, populist patriotism. Financial support of the state for any religious sect, will invariably affect both the dogma of that religious sect, and the politics of the state so that they move ever closer to a single unit seeking control over the nation and the individual.

Rule number three: Secularism is an essential principle of modern liberal republicanism because it protects both the church and the state from each other.

> *"In every country and in every age, the priest has been hostile to liberty. He is always in alliance with the despot, abetting his abuses in return for protection to his own. It is error alone that needs the support of government. Truth can stand by itself."*
>
> ~Thomas Jefferson

Patriotism and faith are two elements of the life of any nation or individual that should never be intertwined. When they are, the result is a state that will begin to claim that its rule is derived from the will of god, and a church that will become the ecclesiastical support for the worst imperial tendencies of the state. When this happens, no republic can long survive.

Republics are always under pressure from non-democratic forces in this world. The secular forces of totalitarianism, and the totalitarian forces of religion are always attempting to undermine the rights of the nation and the individual, thereby subjugating both to their will. We must remember that in no religious sect's vision of heaven is that place a democracy. In fact, heaven is the most totalitarian realm ever created in the human imagination, and the worst apology for religion's general and unwavering support for dictatorship. A god does not put its decisions before any committee.

Both the church and the state possess within themselves the worst drives of the human animal; the lust for power for its own sake, and this is true regardless of your personal opinion of either of these two institutions. Since I have placed that statement in this essay, I feel I must remind the reader that I am not speaking about the deep and sincere faith held by any individual, but the disingenuous propaganda of any institutional church that directs the course of that faith. When the subject is god, people are about faith, churches are about power.

Because of this, republics must be secular in nature. This doesn't place the state in a position above the church, it places the state in a place completely separate from the church. It allows both the church and the state to conduct their business without interference or influence from the other. Secularism, as a foundational principle of republicanism, is not only supposed to prevent favoritism of the state for one religious sect over another, but it is also a mechanism designed to prevent the church from favoring one political party, or viewpoint over another. Therefore, the state cannot offer financial support, nor even comment on the righteousness (or lack thereof) of any religious sect's dogma for any reason. Likewise, no church has the right to speak in favor of any candidate for public office, or any political perspective, or allow its facilities to be used for any political purpose, even if that link is somewhat tenuous.

⸙

I believe that, in large measure, the interests and power of both the church and the state, and the interests of the nation and individuals are always at odds to some degree and are, thereby, in most respects, inversely proportional to one another. This means that as the power of one set of actors increases, the power of the other set of actors must decrease proportionally. Power between these two sets of actors is a zero-sum game, and yet this does not mean that the church and the state, and the nation and thereby the individuals attached to it cannot all flourish within a society.

If we find the proper balance between the two, both the nation, the individuals that comprise it, and the church and state can exist in a healthy symbiosis; all supporting one another and each possessing an appropriate and manageable amount of power in relation to the others. This is the basic socio-political relationship that republics that operate on the democratic process are built to advance; a balance of power between the individual citizens and institutional power structures that govern them.

Each of us is aware that the principle of secularism, of a strict separation of the church and the state has been under attack in this country for at least a couple of generations, and even though it is the forces of the the political right and their "conservative christian" allies that have sought to erase this separation and thereby establish their "free market theocracy," we are all responsible for allowing it to happen.

Every time a person speaks of the good of bringing god into the political life of this nation, and another person within earshot who understands the true nature of patriotism doesn't immediately confront this person, the wall of separation between the church and the state is torn down just a little bit. When someone speaks of such things, it is the responsibility of each of us to remind them that their faith is their business, and since we all have the benefit of living in a secular republic, it has no place in the political life of this nation, or in the life of any individual American.

Every time someone says that "we need to bring prayer back into the public schools," a place where prayer has rightfully never been welcome, and another person doesn't confront this assertion in the strongest possible terms, the wall is demolished a little more. Tell me that there is a Christian who calls for prayer in our public schools who would support a multi-day regimen of prayer in which Christian prayer is observed on one day, Muslim prayer is observed on another day, Buddhist prayer on yet another, and so on down the line, until all of the world's religions are represented in this exercise. I tell you that if such a person exists and speaks up for such a practice, they would be excommunicated from their church forthwith upon discovery of such a rational and blasphemous opinion.

I maintain an acceptance of the ancient dictum that money is the root of all evil; I accept that as truth. I also maintain, perhaps even more fervently, that religion is the root of all hatred. It is the father of all intolerance and the mother of all bigotry.

There may be no more important thread from which our republic hangs than the complete and total separation of the church and the state. More importantly, there may be nothing more intensely tied to our daily freedoms, liberties, our constitutionally guaranteed rights, and the right to worship as we choose, free from unwanted interference than this separation. This is, of course, because both the church and the state have a propensity to overstep their boundaries in all matters of social control, and if we allow them the slightest collusion, the fate of this republic, and the principles of reasoned enlightenment upon which it was founded, may be doomed to an early grave.

PRESUMPTION OF INNOCENCE BEFORE THE LAW

This essay is, by far, the most difficult of the series on which I have chosen to write regarding foundational, philosophical pillars of republicanism. This is for several reasons. First and foremost, it is easy to confuse presumption of innocence before the law with equal treatment before the law. These two are are different, yet closely linked, and both lie at the very core of republicanism as a form of government.

For my purposes in this essay, I will differentiate these two principles in the following manner: presumption of innocence before the law relates to a person's initial contact with the legal system, which is generally with law enforcement, up until the point at which they are tried for an offense of which they are accused, and equal treatment before the law relates to a person's treatment specifically within the court system and after. This essay will not consider the problem of equal treatment before the law, although one could argue (and I would agree) that it deserves its own essay.

Presumption of innocence is also a difficult subject, because unlike the subjects of the previous three essays, The Marketplace of Ideas, Freedom of Conscience and Secularism, which the individual experiences on a level which encompasses the whole of society, the individual experiences presumption of innocence, from a practical perspective, exclusively on an individual level, and only under certain circumstances. This essay will focus partly on how this principle is not only ineptly applied within society, but is also under siege from our own social practices.

Before I actually begin my discussion of the principle of presumption of innocence before the law, I need to write a bit on history education in the United States as our practices in this realm affect, inform, and in many was design how we, as Americans, accept application of this foundational principle.

⚬⚬⚬

I sincerely feel that the United States has never actually embraced the principle of presumption of innocence before the law, regardless of the noble sayings carved into the façades of our courthouses. If you think that a lower-middle class black man in America receives the same presumption of innocence before the law that a middle to upper middle class white American receives, then I am convinced that you believe such a thing only because the reality is too difficult to accept. Such a realization of this inequality would cause catastrophic and irreparable damage to the individual's entire set of universal constructs. Part of the universal construct which envelopes the American mythos is based upon the stated hope surrounding equal and universal application the principle of presumption of innocence. Hope may spring eternal, but the reality does not exist.

There is no sound or valid argument against the fact that white people have, to date, written the history of this country, and so presumption of innocence; enjoyed by white people up and down the socio-economic scale, is propagated as universal in American society. Further to this point, the texts from which our children receive their knowledge of the history of this country in our schools tend to do three things: First, they accentuate and provide illustrative examples of the achievements of white people. Second, they minimize or exclude the accomplishments of people of color. Third, they eliminate, and avoid discussion or illustrative examples of the crimes of white people against other peoples.

One of the results of this is that white-written history tends to claim that the privileges which white people enjoy in this republic either do not actually exist at all, or extend to and are similarly experienced by other, non-white people, thereby negating the existence of white privilege. Another, and more ominous result is that the majority of white people, almost subconsciously resist any restructuring of history education in this country; removing it from its current form, and basing it upon grim reality.

One of the best contemporary efforts to restructure history education in this country and bring it closer to the reality experienced by all racial and ethnic groups in America, is "The 1619 Project." This project is an effort to incorporate illustrative examples of the history of chattel slavery in this country, its effect on the evolution of American society, its long-term effect on the teaching of history in our schools, and most importantly, illuminate the continuing deleterious effect the history of prior enslavement has on black Americans in this society. However, a more detailed and in-depth discussion of racism and its effect on education is for another essay.

In their effort to retain the white-based structure of history and civics education in the United States, the political right has branded education about the role of racism in the evolution of

American society as "Critical Race Theory." Make no mistake, this term was invented by the political right wing, and not those interested in a teaching a holistic, realistic, and racially unbiased history of this country. This allows them to categorize the entirety of eduction regarding the role and effect of racism in America as a single effort with a single goal: to insult and denigrate white people as a whole, to place the blame for the sins of our past onto those alive today, and to minimize the accomplishments and contributions of white people in American culture. In state after state in which the republican party controls the legislature, it is now incredibly difficult, if not outright illegal to teach students about racism at all, especially as it applies the the negative aspects of white involvement in the evolution of American society. This is an attempt to replace 'education' with 'white patriotic education.'

"Patriotic education" of any sort is an extremely dangerous practice in any republic. In order for any republic to flourish, the children must be taught to be critical of their country's history. They must learn to see its flaws as well and its benefits, how it has propelled some, and placed roadblocks in the paths of others. It is only through this critical education that a republic continually evolves and improves its ability to fulfill one of its primary purposes: To provide a stable social and political environment in which power is transferred through an established set of processes from which violence has been removed. "Patriotic education," like so many other practices that the political right is attempting to normalize in American society, is a foundational principle of dictatorship, not republicanism.

Presumption of Innocence and Police Practice

Historically, prior to the rise of republicanism, a person's place before the law was a rather tenuous affair. Before the Age of Enlightenment and Reason, and the illumination of the principles that I have covered in this book, one of the central principles that guided legal systems was 'guilt by association.' Such principles, employed by tyrants, monarchs, and a politically active church, placed the individual accused of any crime in a position of presumed guilt whenever they were suspected of committing and offense outside the parameters of accepted social behavior.

Believe me, I am not so naive to think that a person's place before the law still isn't tenuous at times and especially for various groups, but its tenuous nature is balanced by the rights and liberties possessed by each individual within the Constitution of the republic. Some must scrape and claw to retain these rights and liberties, while others are granted them per se, but at least they are there to be retained.

The bare truth of the matter is that presumption of innocence before the law exists in American society. The sad truth of the matter, is that its existence is not equally distributed between all racial, ethnic, sexually oriented, or gender identifying groups.

The Fourth Amendment to the Constitution of the United States reads:

> "The right of the people to be secure in their persons, houses, papers, and effects, against unreasonable searches and seizures, shall not be violated, and

> *no Warrants shall issue, but upon probable cause,*
> *supported by Oath or affirmation, and particularly*
> *describing the place to be searched, and the persons or*
> *things to be seized."*

The Fifth Amendment to the Constitution of the United States reads:

> *"No Person shall be held to answer for a capital, or*
> *otherwise infamous crime, unless on presentment or*
> *indictment of a Grand Jury, except in cases arising*
> *in the land or naval forces, or in the Militia, when*
> *in actual service in time of War or public danger;*
> *nor shall any person be subject for the same offense to*
> *be twice put in jeopardy of life or limb; nor shall be*
> *compelled in any criminal case to be a witness against*
> *himself, nor be deprived of life, liberty, or property*
> *without due process of law; nor shall private property*
> *be taken for public use without just compensation."*

Qualified Immunity:

There is, perhaps, no practice more abhorrent to the principle of presumption of innocence than that which has become a cornerstone of police practice in America: qualified immunity. In fact, no discussion of the foundational principle of republicanism, presumption of innocence before the law, can proceed without looking critically at this practice. I describe 'qualified immunity' as this: *"Immunity from prosecution for commission of an otherwise criminal act for which another would face arrest and prosecution."* From a theoretical perspective, that is what qualified immunity is.

Think of this, for it is important: When a member of any law enforcement agency kills an innocent person, they are placed on "paid administrative leave." What this boils down to, since they are immune from any accountability for the act, is that when the police kill an innocent person, they receive another two weeks paid vacation. From a practical perspective, this is what qualified immunity has become in America.

The most grotesque aspect of qualified immunity is that it allows the police to set aside presumption of innocence and a person's Fifth Amendment right to not be deprived of their life without due process of law, simply as a matter of convenience. What is, perhaps, the most reprehensible aspect of qualified immunity is that it also allows the police to set themselves as judge, jury, and executioner of an innocent person at any time and not face scrutiny, or be held accountable for their actions. This is true whether one analyzes the effect of taking an innocent person's life on the officer's career, either within their own ranks, or from the broader society. Thankfully, however, we are starting to witness, in America, the development of some cracks in the wall of qualified immunity, and more and more police officers are being held to account for abusive conduct, whether it actually takes the life of an innocent person, or causes them bodily harm.

Qualified immunity, like the sanctified acts of hollow patriotism which infect American society today, are the building blocks of dictatorships, they are not the bricks and mortar of a healthy republic.

The "No-Knock" Warrant

Another building block of dictatorship which has become a common practice in American policing of racial and ethnic minorities is the "no-knock warrant." This allows police, if they feel there may be a threat to their safety within any structure, to simply break into the structure unannounced. They enter in numbers and under a shroud of overwhelming violence, hoping to create chaos among any inside.

I cannot honestly say that a situation could never exist in which the use of a no-knock warrant would be justified. Those situations do exist, but the practice is not applied by American police in American society in a manner that bears any semblance to the extremely rare reality of its appropriateness.

In 2019 the United Stated Department of Homeland Security, in conjunction with the entire range of the United States' intelligence agencies, published a report on the current threats to American National Security. The findings of the American Intelligence Community listed terrorist attacks committed by domestic right-wing extremists as the greatest threat to our national security.

Armed with this information, if you think that police in the United States apply the use of no-knock warrants to the greatest threat to American National Security at the same rate that they apply this principle of dictatorships to the people of color suspected of selling drugs, or, say, cigarettes without a tax stamp, then you should be proud, for you have successfully escaped reality.

It is unfortunate, but as I stated earlier, the application of qualified immunity and the no-knock warrant, as we have seen time and time again, take on a racial and ethnic character. To be quite honest, and to write in complete harmony with the facts of the matter, people of color are abused by the police in this country at a rate white people will never know. Those of us who live within this bubble of white privilege know that our presumption of innocence is guaranteed when confronted with agents of law enforcement. Americans who are not within this demographic have never known presumption of innocence in such a manner.

I read something in 2021 that offered an excellent argument when confronted with a white person who claims that white privilege does not exist, especially when considering police presence and practice. Ask them the following question: "Do you think the police are there to protect you?" When they reply "yes," then you simply inform them that their reply is the voice of white privilege, for no one, other than white people, answer that question in the affirmative. No other racial, ethnic, or gender identifying group other than cis gender white people feel that way, because their experience with law enforcement is very different.

Many years ago, I believe it was in the early to mid 1980's, I heard a news story about a court case in which a judge ruled that if a person exercises their fifth amendment right to remain silent and not incriminate themselves in any supposed wrongdoing, this exercise of a person's constitutional right could be used by law enforcement personnel as an admission of guilt. I was only in my twenties, but I remember seeing the absolute danger this ruling posed to this republic and in particular, the survival of the principle of presumption of innocence.

Both of our Fourth and Fifth Amendment rights under the

constitution are designed to protect the individual from excesses of the state, and to insure this foundational principle of presumption of innocence by making certain that we are secure in our persons against unreasonable and unwarranted search and seizure, and guaranteeing us the right against self incrimination respectively. We cannot allow the exercise of our constitutional rights to be construed as admission of guilt for anything at any time. Guilt for any suspected offense can only be determined by court of competent jurisdiction and a jury of an individual's peers.

Cash Bail System

The last item I would like to briefly discuss in this essay is the cash bail system. The American cash bail system represents an attack on the principle of the presumption of innocence by either extending or denying this constitutional right to individuals based solely on their ability to pay money.

If a person is arrested on suspicion of having broken a law, no matter how minor the breach, or inconsequential to the maintenance of domestic tranquility it may have been, if that person has little or no monetary resources at their disposal, their presumption of innocence before the law disappears. Since they cannot afford to post bond, they are generally incarcerated until trial while they are legally and constitutionally presumed innocent. In a country that arrests and incarcerates people at a rate to which most dictatorships can only aspire, a poor person's time in jail while still presumed innocent can be extensive.

Conversely, if a person is arrested for a major breach of the law that represents a serious attack against maintenance of domestic tranquility and they have ample monetary resources at their disposal, their presumption of innocence remains intact. In all but the rarest of cases, they simply post bond and walk free, regardless of the seriousness of the crime of which they are accused.

Closing Remarks

Presumption of innocence before the law, as a founding principle of this, or any republic that functions on the democratic process, will probably never be applied equally throughout society. Unlike one-party states that can serve only one, or an extremely limited number of groups in its society, republics are designed to serve the broadest range of interests possible, but service of those interests can never be applied equally throughout the entire population. This is not a problem that is particular to republics, or to America, it is a problem particular to humans.

Lastly, if the United States has ever tried to fully integrate the foundational principle of presumption of innocence before the law into the practiced legal traditions of this republic, it has strayed so far from such an effort that most people who consider our history from a needed, critical perspective, understand that once basic human rights, or closer to the truth; the rights enjoyed by white people, started to be extended to all persons within society, any true equality of application would be well nigh impossible. Armed with this knowledge, we seem to have then decided that lip service is all this principle would receive.

Still, we must continue to pursue this ever elusive goal of

equal distribution of the rights and liberties guaranteed to each of us under our Constitution. It is only through this pursuit of the perfection of the adoption and application of the foundational principles I am discussing in these essays: The Marketplace of Ideas, Freedom of Conscience, Secularism, Presumption of Innocence Before the Law, and The Rule of Law, that we progress ever so slowly toward a more perfect union and preserve what little domestic tranquility we have left to us.

THE RULE OF LAW

This essay on the rule of law is the last in my series of five on the foundational principles of republicanism as a form of government. "The rule of law" is a concept expressed in four very small words of one syllable each. It is easy to say and extremely popular in the current news cycle, but the heart of this principle can be obscured behind layers of interpretation and preferences.

I think it is important to note that this essay was started in September, 2022, in the aftermath of the FBI's execution of a search warrant of former president Donald Trump's residence in Mar-a-Lago, Florida. I work on these essays for several months each, writing on consecutive days, then not doing so for several days in a row, or even a week. I feel this keeps the essay well rounded, as I step back and take time to reread and think about what I have written previously, and then proceed to amend and expand.

On this particular date, September 19th, 2022, the US Federal Appeals Court struck down part of judge Aileen Cannon's ruling in which she barred the Department of Justice from analyzing the cache of documents seized in the execution of the warrant mentioned above until such time as the Special Master she appointed had an opportunity to review the entire trove of documents seized, and I discuss Judge Cannon's rulings on this matter in slightly greater detail later in this essay.

Since the time at which I initially wrote the paragraph above, the Federal Appeals court has completely struck down and vacated Judge Cannon's ruling.

Although I do not feel I should have to say that the rule of law in this country is under attack like never before in our history, I suppose that I should say so (and I am), and then illuminate several of the ways in which this assault on the rights and liberties of the people in this country is proceeding. Therefore, I shall say, unequivocally, we are facing a crisis in this country in which the survival of this republic, and everything for which it has stood, but as yet has failed to achieve for the people of this world, is at stake.

⁂

In the post World War Two political environment, as humanity took a deep breath and tried to figure out how we were to move forward without again facing the type of massive conflict from which we had just emerged, two major questions faced the world.

First, how were we to manage and prevent further use of the new, massively destructive atomic weaponry developed by the United States and used against the Japanese Empire, which was certain to be produced and deployed by other nation-states. The world's political leaders in this post-war environment, in which establishing a durable peace was paramount, understood what the use of these weapons would mean for life on this planet: an end to it.

The second question was a reflection on what had happened, politically, to the people under the governments of the Axis

Powers, especially focused on the people of Germany. The question which gnawed at the soul of humanity, and specifically of Western cultures, was this: How could the culture that had produced Beethoven, Bach, Goethe, Dürer and other, innumerable, artists, philosophers, and great thinkers come so fully under the sway of someone like Hitler and the barbaric philosophy of the Nazi regime? Also, having come under that sway, how could they then commit acts so horrific, and so heinous against people solely because they were different than them? How could they brutalize and then kill tens of millions of people for no reason whatsoever? This is what became known as "The German Question."

The Holocaust was something for which the German government and the German people had to answer before the world, and though a few major actors escaped justice and the world's retribution for what they did, most of those involved paid with their lives for their roles in it, but another aspect of The German Question is how could the German people also allow the rule of law within the fledgeling Weimar Republic to become so subverted and twisted that it existed solely to serve the purposes of the Nazi regime?

This aspect of The German Question is what we must examine for ourselves if we are to preserve our own republic and guard its existence into the foreseeable future, because the real danger to any nation regarding the rule of law is not that their body of laws will be completely swept aside and replaced with a different body of laws; this circumstance lies fully within the realm of successful revolutionary movements, but that both the laws in effect and new laws added to the body will be subverted and weaponized for the power purposes of the regime.

Those who felt comfortable believing they had found concrete answers to The German Question in the eccentricities of German culture, especially in the United States, resolved themselves to a truth they created for their own comfort: "It can't happen here." My dear readers, not only can it happen here, but it is happening here. The Rule of Law, which has carried this republic through innumerable trials and tribulations for almost 250 years, as I write today, is under threat like at no other time in our history.

To be quite honest, if the forces arrayed on the far right in this country have their way with our republic, it will no longer exist in any form recognizable to those who founded it, those who, over the centuries, died for it, or those, who even today, seek to preserve it. It will, however, be recognizable to the racists and fascists of the past, the Mullahs of present day Iran, president Xi of China, the Kim family of North Korea, and the Butcher of Moscow, Vladimir Putin.

⋘⋙

Perhaps there is no greater and more important philosophical pillar that supports the republican form of government than the rule of law. This concept, designed to create a basic equality amongst every single member of society, may very well be the absolute cornerstone of republicanism as a form of government. It really is the sine qua non of any real modern liberal republic that functions on the democratic process.

In this regard, I wrote the following brief note when thinking about the content of this essay:

"Republics differ from dictatorships at their very core; whether those dictatorships be monarchies, in which those who rule claim that right because it is given to them through their ancestors and god, or civil and military dictatorships in which those who rule claim that right through their overwhelming possession of access to the tools of violence. This is because the laws of any republic are paramount in that society, and no person or persons, whether they be presidents, would-be monarchs, or want-to-be tyrants are above those laws."

The essence of this difference lies in the decentralized manner in which the laws that govern society are made. In dictatorships, the laws that govern citizens and residents of a country are made in a highly centralized manner by a very small, select group of individuals. I understand that the person reading this essay is probably thinking: "Are you trying to tell me that our laws in the United States of America are not made in a highly centralized manner, by a very small, select group of individuals? Yes, I am, and here is why.

In a republic that functions on the democratic process, the mass electorate has both the right and, in my view, the responsibility to periodically elect those who will make the laws that will govern their society. Those elected officials, being the small, select group of individuals that they are, will either continue to enforce the current body of laws, or modify that current body either through addition of new laws, or subtracting laws from that body. The official's performance in this respect is then reviewed by the electorate on a regularly scheduled basis, and the individuals are either retained in office, or expelled through the democratic process. This is modern liberal republicanism as it is meant to function.

In non-constitutional monarchies, and civil and religious dictatorships, this opportunity does not really exist. There may be elections, but the results are known before the votes are cast. There may be elections, but the persons who are the primary challengers to the regime are sitting in prison cells on election day. There may be elections, but violence at polling stations is rampant, and the bulk of the electorate often stay home in order to stay alive. Add to this that in civil and military dictatorships, there is no such thing as a legitimate and active 'opposition party,' so the actions of the regime are not challenged within the government itself.

The rule of law, as it has evolved from the Age of Enlightenment to the twenty-first century, exists as a bulwark against the aspirations of monarchs and tyrants alike. It is, on the one hand, quite simple, and yet on the other hand, it is quite a complicated affair. As always in the operations of humans, there is a vast chasm between the theoretical proposition, and the application of that theory within society. As I stated in the essay on the presumption of innocence before the law:

> *"If you think that a lower-middle class black man in America receives the same presumption of innocence before the law that a middle to upper middle class*

white American receives, then I am convinced that
you believe such a thing only because the reality is too
difficult to accept."

Unfortunately, the same is true of the rule of law. No one is above the law, and no one is below it, but if you are poor, especially poor and identify as a member of a racial, ethnic, or sexually oriented minority in America, would will, more often than not, find yourself on the short end of it.

In my opinion, the following statement expresses what the rule of law means on a theoretical level and should mean on a practical level.

"In a society that adheres to the philosophical
proposition of the rule of law, those people who possess
vast amounts of wealth and power are, and must be,
held to the same standards of conduct as all other
members of that society, even those who possess no
wealth or power. Likewise, if you are a member of
that same society, and you possess little or no wealth or
power, you are, and must be, guaranteed access to the
same protections under the law as every other member
of that society, especially those who possess vast amounts
of wealth and power."

In a republic that functions on the democratic process and adheres to the rule of law, the law rules, people do not. Government officials, whether they are elected or appointed, are in their positions solely for the purpose of administering and defending the rule of law, and within that task, the body of laws that govern the society of which they are members. In a republic such as ours, the core laws that govern our society are contained in our Constitution. Beyond that, they are contained in statutory law, passed by legislatures, signed into law by chief executives, and then, if challenged, upheld as constitutional by the courts.

Republics are always under pressure from the forces of totalitarianism in this world, and the United States of America witnessed the application of this pressure in late 2020 and early 2021. Donald Trump, his sycophants in Congress, and his followers in the far right white power movement, demonstrated on January 6th, 2021 exactly how far want-to-be tyrants will go to secure power, even in the United States of America.

Benjamin Franklin is rumored to have warned us about the constant dangers any republic faces. There is an episode that has been related many times, though, as far as I know, not confirmed, that when Mr. Franklin emerged from the constitutional convention the crowd waiting outside asked him what type of government he and the other delegates had created for them, to which he is rumored to have said: "A republic, if you can keep it."

"If you can keep it."

Everyone reading this essay must realize that what happened on January 6th, 2021, was an attempted coup d'état in the United States; an attempt, through violence, to seize power in this country in direct opposition to the will of the American electorate. The coup attempt failed to secure power for Donald Trump and his base on the extreme right in this country, but it did succeed in some aspects.

First, it galvanized the vast majority of the white power movement in this country behind Trump as the beleaguered and persecuted messiah who speaks for them. Second, it brought the conspiracy theory adherents of Q-Anon and their universe of fantastical beliefs fully into the mainstream of the republican party. Third, and most importantly, it disrupted, for the first time in the modern history of this republic, the peaceful transfer of power from one administration to the next. Trump and his followers did not prevent the transfer of power, but they introduced violence into the process. Now, through their control, if not outright ownership of the republican party, the far right, MAGA, Q-Anon adherents are trying to normalize this violence within our democratic process.

This attempted coup was a planned and organized assault on our democratic processes and directly targeted the rule of law in the United States. To be sure, corruption of any sort among government officials is always an assault on the rule of law, and neither republicans nor democrats are immune to the lure of wealth and power that does not belong to them. Corruption is an assault on the rule of law because it demonstrates that because of their wealth and power, these people believe that the law does not apply to them.

This is not uncommon in societies all over the world, even today. Various groups on both the right and the left in the United States will say "We are a nation of laws" when such a stance suits their power needs, and both will seek a path around those laws when they feel it necessary. Yes, we are a nation of laws, but that statement is only true if we accept the rule of law, and acceptance of the rule of law must be, from both a theoretical and a practical perspective, a complete and total acceptance, for it will determine the very nature of a people's government and society, and how those two elements of the life of the nation-state evolve.

⚬✖⚬

As I stated early in this essay, I will now turn our attention to the ruling of Judge Aileen Cannon regarding the case of the Department of Justice's search of former president, Donald Trump's residence in Florida, seeking return of the American People's property. I would suggest that anyone interested in the basic tenets of the rule of law in a society and the role of the courts in that realm read Judge Cannon's decision. The entire ruling, and the various cases referenced within it, will alert the reader to the fact that Judge Cannon was seeking a way, by any means necessary, to grant the Plaintiff's request to any degree possible. The case references therein are tenuous, at best, but pages nine and ten of the twenty-four page ruling mark the point at which the Judge decides to completely forego application of the law in favor of the Plaintiff.

I have included three excerpts from Judge Cannon's ruling for review in this essay.

Excerpt #1

> *"...Further, the Plaintiff is at risk of suffering injury from the government's retention and potential use of privileged materials in the course of a process that, thus far, has been closed off to the Plaintiff and that has*

raised at least some concerns as to its efficacy, even if
inadvertently so…"

It is incredibly important to realize that in the above excerpt, the judge immediately steps beyond merely supporting the Plaintiff's motion, and her intent to grant at least partial relief, but ventures into the realm of supporting the Plaintiff in all aspects of the legal jeopardies facing the Plaintiff outside of her courtroom and the specific case before her.

When she writes that the process had "thus far been closed off to the Plaintiff," she is stating an absolute falsehood that she knew was false when she wrote it. When she writes of the Department of Justice's investigations "has raised some concerns as to its efficacy, even if inadvertently so" she assumes the position of support for the Plaintiff as a general rule, outside of the strict confines of the motion before her. Also, as we will see in the other excerpts, there is no reference to any applicable law.

Excerpt #2

"…Finally, Plaintiff has claimed injury from the threat
of future prosecution and the serious, often indelible
stigma associated therewith. As the Richey court wrote
'a wrongful indictment is no laughing matter, it often
works a grievous, irreparable harm to the person
indicted. The stigma cannot be easily erased. In the
public mind, the blot on a man's escutcheon, resulting
from such public accusation of wrongdoing is seldom
wiped out by a subsequent judgment of not guilty.

*Frequently, the public remembers the accusation, and
still suspects guilt, even after an acquittal'..."*

In this excerpt, judge Cannon intends to grant the Plaintive
relief based solely on the potential stigma that might occur if the
Plaintiff were to face indictment and prosecution for criminal
offenses arising out of this investigation, as well as crimes of which
he may be accused in the future in investigation that are part of
the case before her.

Again, as in excerpt #1, there is no reference to applicable law,
only her blatant desire to see that the Plaintiff will not suffer any
potential future embarrassment which may arise from a criminal
indictment in the case before her, were the government to use
material that may rightly be considered the Plaintiff's personal
property. Lastly, the embarrassment suffered by any party to a legal
proceeding is not the concern of the judge presiding over the case.

Excerpt #3

*"...As a function of the Plaintiff's former position as
President of the United States, the stigma associated
with the subject seizure is in a league of its own. A
future indictment, based to any degree on material
that ought to be returned, would result in reputational
harm of a decidedly different order of magnitude..."*

In this excerpt, Judge Cannon decides to completely disregard
any semblance of impartiality and clearly states that, in her opinion,
the Plaintiff should be granted relief solely based upon prior

employment that would appear on his resume. Yet again, there is nothing in this excerpt, or in the entire ruling that references applicable law.

The above excerpts from Judge Cannon's ruling in this matter are important for several reasons, because they highlight what the role of the judicial branch of our government, at any level, should be, and stand as an example of the injustice society as a whole can suffer when judges decide to serve a master other than the Constitution and our accompanying body of statutory laws.

Judge Cannon's entire ruling also demonstrates what can happen when the court decides to forego its role of interpreting the merits of any case based upon applicable law and decide, instead, to reach decisions based upon the personal preferences of the presiding judge when they decide to serve a master other than the one they swore an oath to defend when they assumed the office they hold. Fortunately, the American system of appeal and review worked as it should in this case, and the appeals court of competent jurisdiction completely struck down and vacated Judge Cannon's ruling in this matter.

⚬⚬⚬

The role of the judicial branch of our government is to act as the last bastion of the equitable application of the rule of law in this country. I say 'equitable application,' because the principle of judicial review, established in *Marbury v. Madison*, results from the predilection of legislatures and chief executives to draft, execute, and implement laws that are either not equitable at their conception, or not applied equitably among all members of society. They often either target various groups and subject them to persecution based upon frivolous beliefs and/or preferences, or set the rule of law aside for the benefit of certain groups, offering them special treatment within the body of statutory law. The judiciary is charged with making certain that neither of these two scenarios are allowed to infect our society's legal tradition, and that, as I stated earlier in this essay:

> *"In a society that adheres to the philosophical proposition of the rule of law, those people who possess vast amounts of wealth and power are, and must be, held to the same standards of conduct as all other members of that society, even those who possess no wealth or power. Likewise, if you are a member of that same society, and you possess little or no wealth or power, you are, and must be, guaranteed access to the same protections under the law as every other member of that society, especially those who possess vast amounts of wealth and power."*

The rule of law, so central to republicanism as a form of government, like the other topics discussed in these essays, is both extremely fragile and, at the same time, quite durable. Its fragility stems from its susceptibility to the machinations of want-to-be tyrants, yet it derives its durability from its deep roots in the history of this republic and the dedication of all but a few people who have chosen to serve the public trust. Whether one sees its fragility or its durability, we must defend the rule of law without thought of, or care for, the cost, and we depend on all three branches of our government to insure that the rule of law is, indeed, defended at all costs.

As I stated earlier in this essay, the threat to the rule of law in this country is not that our body of laws will be completely swept aside, but that they will be subverted and weaponized to serve the desires of a single group of people led by a would-be dictator. Unfortunately, vast numbers of the republican party in this country, from non-politically active rank and file members, all the way to United States Senators, see the the rule of law, applied universally in a just and equitable manner, as standing in the way of their power aspirations.

I do not think I can express strongly enough what a very dangerous time this is for this country, because we are now in a time in which a demagogue has used his moderately honed sense of salesmanship to assume control of one of the two major political parties in this country. His base of followers, from the uneducated (who he loves so much) to the well educated, from the poor to the professionally successful, all exist within the boundaries of the fascist, racist, white supremacist, white power movement in this country, and they will subvert and weaponize our legal traditions for their own ends if they are successful in gaining power.

Even though we depend on our government to defend the rule of law, in the end it is our government that will depend on us to defend this cornerstone of republicanism. If we do not do so, then the future of this nation; of its citizens, of the non-citizens who live under its protections, and indeed, the entire world will turn very bleak very fast.

POSTSCRIPT

In the preceding essays, I have tried to convey not only the importance of the principles laid out in each, but also how each is under attack in contemporary America. In fact, republicanism throughout the West is under attack from elements of the far right present in every culture in Europe. The reasons vary, but they can all be traced to a very basic sense of racism that does not trace its origins to Europe per se, but rather to every human culture. The problem for us is that the white power movement, global in its scope and completely networked over that same globe, is rising in its visibility and volume.

This rise in the visibility and promulgation of national far right, white power movements is exacerbated by the dictatorships of what is commonly referred to as the Third and Fourth Worlds. The governments that rule these countries without restraint on the corruption within the government as well as the cruelty they impose upon their citizens, have caused a mass exodus of good people who merely want to make good lives for themselves and their families. The fact that these people, in the European context, are racially and ethnically not European, combined with their shear numbers has provided fodder for the ever-present far right, racist, white power political movements throughout Europe and the United States.

This situation is not new to republics, for as I have stated several times in these essays, they are always under attack from the forces of totalitarianism on both the far right and the far left. In twenty-first century United States, the greatest threat to this republic now emanates from the political right. Elements of fascism and white supremacy have always been present in America, but now, since the rise of trumpism within the American right wing, these extremist views have been adopted by the republican party, which not only gives them comfort and succor, but also engages in a continuous effort to legitimize them within the American political debate.

As we have witnessed, the evolution of any republic that functions on the democratic process moves inexorably toward greater inclusion, greater liberty, and greater influence of all demographic groups within society. It is the politics of the far right which seeks to turn back our clocks; to place this country and, indeed, the world into Monsieur Wells' time machine and remove us to some mythical distant past, when things were better, simpler, exclusion was the order of the day, and only a select, racially homogeneous few had the right to determine what is best for all. This is the greatest of the characteristic properties of fascist, racial supremacist, white power movements. They are always based in a mythological history in which its adherents believe that they were once at the summit of the social and political pyramid in their society.

In relation to this, I suppose I should place here a comment about the differences between far left and far right movements, because once either of these political movements gains power, they are essentially the same. Whether it is a communist movement of the far left, or a fascist, racial or ethnic supremacist movement of the far right, once they possess political power in any country, they become almost indistinguishable from one another. They both attempt to assume vast amounts of control over almost every aspect of the individual citizen's life.

There are vast differences in their core propaganda, but there are still, within such, extensive similarities. Both focus their appeal on those who may feel downtrodden and left behind by a society that has forgotten them. The differences lie in other aspects of their philosophical appeal.

Among other things, movements of the far left seek to appeal to the middle and lower socio-economic strata in society by highlighting economic injustice that is present in all societies. The disparities in wealth and its accompanying political power that are always present provide fodder to the far left's call for economic justice as well as greater inclusion of all demographic groups in the national economy. In short, the propaganda of Communist movements looks toward a brighter future for the nation by looking forward to a potential future that has yet to come.

Opposite this, movements of the far right seek to appeal to the middle and lower socio-economic strata of the dominant racial and ethnic demographic groups within society. They appeal to this group's sense of loss of power, influence, and control as society has moved toward greater inclusion of previously marginalized groups. When they make their appeal to any sense of economic injustice, they invariably make that appeal by focusing on the wealth acquired by a racial or ethnic minority within society, thereby creating an enemy upon which their adherents can focus their hatred. Stated simply, the propaganda of political movements of the far right look toward a brighter future for the nation by looking backward to a mythological past that must be resurrected.

In contemporary American society, this effort by the white power movement has assumed the moniker of "replacement theory." The proponents of this proposition claim that white Americans, who used to hold all or most of the political power in the United States, are being replaced by mongrel races and inferior ethnic groups, and that eventually, white people will find themselves completely marginalized in American society, if not outlawed altogether.

In either case, political movements of both the far right and the far left are enemies of republics that function on the democratic process.

⚬✖⚬

In the final calculation, we must, as a society, decide how we will protect our republic from those who would carve its date of death on history's tombstone. To be certain, we have many options available to us in doing so. First, we can engage in some sort of violent civil war against the far right, or the far left in this country, but that option will stand very little chance of producing anything that even remotely resembles a just society. Second, we can call what is known as this 'great American experiment' a failure, dissolve the United States as we know it into at least two completely sovereign states, and give the far right back their precious Confederacy; they already have their flag, their heroes, and their villains; all they need now are actual political and geographic borders.

Although this option seems rather palatable to many, the

mechanisms for doing so are rather complicated, and would take a minimum of five years to complete. Also, The United States would not be able to allow the Confederacy to assume control of any portion of its nuclear arsenal. I may, in the near future, compose an essay on the required processes for dissolving the United States into two separate and equal nation-states, because to be quite honest, I have given the idea a fair amount of thought. There are times when I believe that dissolution of this republic is the only workable long-term solution to the hardened political divide in this country, but these are solely contained within moments of political despair and vanish rather quickly.

Complete political and social dissolution notwithstanding, if we are to maintain the United States in its current configuration, and not allow ourselves to be drawn into either years of violent social and political upheaval, or a complete disassembly of our republic, then there is only one option: education. We must educate our youth on the principles that form the foundations of modern, liberal republicanism. We must begin this education when they are in the earliest grades, and continue it, at the very least, through the end of their secondary education.

Their education on the principles of republicanism cannot be contained in elective courses, it must be a continually required portion of their curriculum. Of course, in addition to this required curriculum on the principles of republicanism, greater, in depth education on not only the five principles contained in this book, but others, as well as the philosophical foundations from which these principles arose should always be available as elective courses. As with all things that either propel a society into the future, try to hold it in a state of artificial stasis in which progress is halted, or worst of all, try to remove that society out of the present and place it somewhere in the past, education of our youth is the key.

The question then becomes, can this be done? Of course it can be done, but developing a standardized national curriculum would be problematic at best, and states in which the legislatures are controlled by the republican party would never agree to such a thing. Not only because it would represent federal intrusion into a field that they consider to be fully within the purview of the states, but these principles now run counter to the direction in which this party has been moving for almost forty years. This situation is exacerbated by the fact that the person who leads this party is blatantly calling for termination of our constitutional protections of checks and balances and separation of powers, so that he can somehow be reinstated into the office of President of the United States.

This effort to overturn the free and fair presidential election of 2020 is not being condemned by every member of the republican party. In fact, almost no republican officials at the state and federal level have even ventured to criticized these anti-American remarks at all, and this, really, is the most troubling and dangerous aspect of the environment surrounding this former president's remarks.

⁕

"A republic, if you can keep it." These words, reportedly spoken by Benjamin Franklin, after our Constitution was drafted and agreed upon by the delegates to the convention, ring true every single day in the life of any republic that functions on the democratic process and adheres to the rule of law. They are always under assault from anti-democratic forces, just as the life and teachings of Jesus are under attack from 'conservative' American Evangelical Christianity.

The principles that laid the foundation for our republic, of which the marketplace of ideas, freedom of conscience, secularism, presumption of innocence before the law, and the rule law are but five, must be defended each day if we are to keep this republic. I am not talking about policy, I am talking about principles. Policy and principles are so different that one could consider them to exist in geometrically parallel universes. Policy is always on a pendulum that moves from left, to right, and then back again. In doing so, it creates a perpetual system of shifting alliances, coalitions, and compromises that propel us, ever so slowly, but inexorably and inevitably toward that elusive 'more perfect union.' The principles upon which our modern liberal republic was founded must never be placed on such a pendulum.

Our best means to keep our precious, purposefully inefficient governmental system is to adhere to the five principles contained in the essays in this book, demand that our elected officials adhere to them as well, and to continually educate our youth on their essential importance to the survival of our country. If we, as a nation, do these things, our precious republic will last well beyond the foreseeable future. If we do not, then we will find ourselves in a system and a situation that will crush the hopes of freedom and liberty for us, and really, for this entire planet.

Printed in the United States
by Baker & Taylor Publisher Services